# The 13th Floor:
# Step into Anxiety

Poems by Steve Gerson

Spartan
Press

Spartan Press

Kansas City, MO

spartanpress.com

Spartan
Press

Cover and title page art: Larry Thomas

Author photo: Tom Tarnowski

"Among America's most prolific, penetrating, and prescient poets, Steve Gerson deftly delivers yet again with his latest volume, *The 13th Floor: Step into Anxiety* with Jeremiah-like lamentations. Brilliantly, even luminously drawn, this collection contains Gerson's typically elegant verses but also masterful flash stories and abbreviated musings. Subject matters are of the micro and macro level, intimate and not, pertaining to personal or global occurrences, which exude permanence or evanescence. In trademark fashion, Gerson artfully explores cutting-edge events ranging from the pandemic to endless tumult in the Near East and Putin's war in Ukraine to Americana at its most moving, poignant, wistful, terrifying, and, yes, hopeful. Thus, the reader encounters the rapidly transmuting virus but also another deadly epidemic: that of random shootings with far-too-young victims. Included too are meaningful stories of loss pertaining to relationships, economic distress, and the human condition itself, imperiled by climatic catastrophe. But then so are significant generational experiences and those clearly distinctive during this 'time of anxiety' when 'even peace is frightening.' Particularly fascinating and affecting are the dedication, 'Black Spring,' 'In this time of anxiety,' 'New Word,' 'Our Prayers,' 'The Existential Sundering of OK Boomer and Gen Z,' and 'The memoir of no one special.'"

-Dr. Robert C. Cottrell, *The Activist 1960s: Striving for Political and Social Empowerment in America*

"'So I turn on my smartphone to mute distraction.' 'Want to eat some stress?' Could there be a more accurate statement and subsequent question (approximately 20 pages apart) summarizing today's society and our hyperfocus on the constant flood of information? Although sad but true, Gerson calls to attention the innumerable factors in life that can and do lead to anxiety. Even for those of us who are privileged, the world in which we live is challenging. The demands of life are simply ongoing and often unpredictable. In reading Gerson's chapbook, we learn that at least we're not alone."

-Dr. Stefani Buchwitz, Director, Self Graduate Programs, University of Kansas

"In these troubling times, it helps to feel less alone, more connected, and seen by others. Steve Gerson's chapbook does that – his depictions of anxiety, depression, loss, and fear help give the fleeting emotions that drift through your thoughts a space to breathe. In a series of vignettes, his attention to time's inexorable march forward allows you to step out of your own world and step into a very real depiction of the unreal. Take this pause as a way to reflect on your own experience. Let his torment lessen your own. Steve's beautiful, sometimes haunting, sometimes humorous depictions of other lives each transport you to another space, another time, and another existence. His artistic and evocative expressions of feeling and emotion leave you thoughtful and more fulfilled."

> -Stacy Harken, JD, Information Architect/
> Technical Writer, Garmin Industries

"*The 13th Floor* by Steve Gerson is a book of poems, flash stories, and musings that tackles the modern paradox of loneliness in modern life, with all its opulence. Depression is rampant with undercurrents of latent anxiety. This work cuts through all the noise that comes with existing in a fast-paced society. And in this exploration, Gerson takes the reader on a hilarious ride that is pure schadenfreude. The genius of this work is that it is not an attack. Gerson does not preach. Rather, it is a feel-good rollick through everyday musings that will leave the reader smiling and pausing to connect intensely with Gerson's imagery. This book is a meditation on what we need to laugh at in these anxious times. *13th Floor* is the magic bullet to smile and deserves a permanent seat on the coffee table with the iPhone and the laptop."

> -Rob Titus, JD, Titus Law Firm

# Acknowledgments:

**Poems:**

"Is everyone screaming?," "The fish that ate the worm that
   swallowed the" / *Mercury Retrograde*

"Dad's Boots" / *Vermilion*

"Who am I Today" / *Panoplyzine*

"The Seven Sins of Suburbaniacs," "Tattooed straight lines
   not sufficing" / *In Parentheses*

"Self Portrait as Sea Surge," "Beneath the Sea's Swell the
   Psyche" / *Wingless Dreamer*

"Black Spring" / *Untenured*

"In this time of anxiety," "Flayed" / *Scapegoat*

"Recipe for Anxiety" / *Nat1*

"Cancer Triptych"    / *Rainbow Poems*

"New Word" / *New Note*

**Flash Stories**:

"Them" / *New Note*

"A Truck in Snow" / *Zoetic Press*

"Shell" / *Leon Literary Review*

"Sepia" / *Quibble*

"And the morning sun trailed her bus in shadows,"
   "Prophesies" / *CafeLit*

"Love/Loveless"  / *The Bookends Review*

"Pale Green and Garnet" / *NiftyLit*

"Not Today," "Maybe hope," "Llano Estacado"
   / *The Dead Mule School of Southern Literature*

"Lurking"  / *Southern Florida Poetry Journal*

"Waxing Moon"  / *In Parentheses*

"When fields bloom dust"  / *Underwood Press*

"Progress" / *Snapdragon*

"The Existential Sundering of OK Boomer and Gen Z,"
   "Sunset diorama" / *Big Bend Literary Magazine*

**Micro Musings**:

"Poems find light through broken glass" / *Vermilion*

"Ingesting eclipses" / *Abstract*

# TABLE OF CONTENTS

Introduction

## Poems

## Flash Stories

# Micro Musings

Anxiety!

We're living in weird and challenging times. Maybe we
always are, the human condition. War, gun violence, fear,
stress, and strife. This hybrid chapbook of poems, micro,
and flash examines divorce, disease, prejudice, uncertainty,
aging, and a whole maelstrom of angst, not from a historical
perspective but from a visceral reaction.

Step off the 13th floor elevator with me . . . into anxiety.

For Sharon, always
Here's what I have
my hand upon the small of your back

to touch you as softly as a scent of rain
my arm in yours to ward off roots

that threaten to strain your stride
my lips upon yours to taste your breath

as yearning as our future
as fulfilling as our past

my eyes alert to all we have been
the dark of mine the light in yours

my heart completely engorged
pumping delight and thankfulness

these are what I have
to celebrate the wonder that is you

Poems

# Is everyone screaming?

1.

Sitting in a car dealership waiting room.
Surrounded by noise. Five TVs.
All on different stations.
Two sportscasts with competing pundits.
Screaming opposing views
on who's the best quarterback.
This day week month season career lifetime eternity.
Three news stations with pundits screaming.
About conspiracies the end of democracy
the end of earth in climate catastrophe
the end of the end of the end.
Six car sales staff perfecting bonhomie.
As if you're their bestie and the last gas guzzling
$60,000 car on the showroom floor
is calling your name like a pet store pooch
with sad eyes.

2.

So I turn on my smartphone to mute distraction.
And get infiltrated by incoming spam email updates.
A sexual-satisfaction aid a request for donations
to support candidates who alone can save the world
a plea to pay back my school loan from 1978.
So to escape spam I check my social.
And get bombarded by incoming TikTok Tweet IM
Snapchat Insta influencers.
Kardashian-smashing flashing thrashing trashing.

3.

My ears are bee stung.

I'm anaphylactic and gasping.

My head is clanging like

the jump-ship bells on the Titanic.

The air raid sirens at Pearl Harbor (ooh ahh ooh ahh).

The fire trucks blaring on 9/11 towards two buildings

in smoke and lost innocence.

The sound of a tyrant bellowing bellicose beseechments.

To overthrow a government.

Existential. Epochal. Noise.


4.

I'm ready to pull my ear buds.

Oedipus-blind myself.

Plato-cave dwell.

Help!

Get me out!

# The fish that ate the worm that swallowed the

Ever feel full? I mean really topped off
fed up gill stuffed data engorged?
I saw a photo in a doctor's office waiting
room of an Everglade's boa constrictor
swallowing a freshwater crocodile and
exploding from the effort. Too much food,
too little gut. Well, that's me.
Swollen to bursting from scirocco plumes
of tsunami swales of 24/7 newscasts
special commissions investigating insurrection
theories flak-jacketed correspondents
covering a war here a war there
and/or/even more endemic pandemics
starring bat infected monkey pox. My brain
is a detonating mushroom cloud of
information drilled into my ear
and other orifices by multi-modal media
delivered through diverse platforms
as I walk talk drive eat sleep read
seed speed plead needed or not.
I'm full—up to here, neither enlightened
nor comforted nor nutritionally improved.
Instead, I feel like an ice floe-leaping polar bear
that ate a fish that ate a worm that swallowed
the Earth in orbit and all the planets crashing down
from oxygen deprivation filmed live at 6:00 pm
by a crew on a stranded ship in the world's low tide.

## Facial Recognition

You think you see me
walking through a checkpoint

know me through geometry
gauging distance between

my eyes nose lips chin
plotting a fractal faceprint

I barely see myself
in mirrors reflecting mirrors

versions of me
me v. 1.0, v. 2.0

standing between parents
generations behind me

like migrants disembarking
in Kodachrome sepia

like migrants crossing
border barriers

sliced by barbed wire
then generations beyond me

blooming a blurred future
myself a hologram quavering

a light field lightly drawn
from multitudes

but you think you see
the shadows of my fears

the infinite possibilities
of my dreams?

## Dad's Boots

My dad's Nocona cowboy boots
vermin-skinned steel-toed
lie in my basement beneath
six cans of used paint mostly
black a child's broken toy
lost when a forgotten niece
visited dried flower arrangements
from a failed Thanksgiving
petals dropping like panicked
dreams the boot shafts tightly
stitched adorned with predatory
red tail hawks perched
each talon pinioning prey
on faded cacti the spines
exclamation points shrieking
heels rundown and dirt-caked
a barbed wire scar bisecting
the left instep like the serrated edge
of a thunderstorm the boots the color
of bad blood

## Don't turn away

Don't turn away.

That's what you do, even if the sky
is pink/blue, certainly when

there are clouds,
our life gloaming.

You see only the darkest
trees in the forest, the ones shaded

and shrunken from dimmed light
disappearing, though others are

in full bloom, their leaves reaching
toward wonder.  On our dark days,

where rivers ice and birds hush,
their songs muffled in molting,

you embrace the hollow.
It's only moments, those shadows,

can't you see?  Where a cloud wanders,
and even the clouds shift shapes.

If we're, you and I, apart in thought,
and I look right while you look left,

that's not us defined in infinity
of sky. Our distances are as

transient as watercolors washing.
Feel the now of our palette.

Embrace our shades, our variegation.
Hear the trill of the warbler's song.

Don't turn away.

# Who am I Today

Yesterday I needed
to be strong a gull
flying against gale
headwinds buffeted
by wind shears grayness
graying in turbulence
she was hurting and
I needed/wanted to
be wings

Last week I was
weakened in the face of
24/7 bitter blizzard newscasts
hurling blisters like
sandstorms arid epithets
of dissension divisiveness
and I leaned on her
she a palm tree rooted
in an oasis of heart

Last year amid viral
wasps stinging with
spores amid the contagion
of earworm drilling vlogging
blogging I was a reeling
tweetstorm a mental
hurricane of barometric
upheaval

Tomorrow I'll invent
my next self my next
sense of being needed
to confront the whatever
life invites a new
roiling endemic an
old familial relationship
requiring massaging
I'll knead plead reseed

## The Seven Sins of Suburbaniacs

He and she live on Morning Star Drive their neighbors
on Moonglow Lane the east to west constellations running
parallel but crossing the north to south
streets where other his and hers live on
Primrose Terrace and Daisy Avenue
the botanicals sweet smelling in their
coloration all the neighbors in harmony but
secrets they fail to share uproot the florals and
send the stars out of alignment
for within the well adorned pastel homes
manicured lawns in military precision
saluting swings and slides tatty flags patio grills
trikes on driveways trees in
matching designer suits with handwashed SUVs
washed by paid hands lies
a stew of banality with bestial ingredients
like his absorption with the gleam
of new gizmos bought at premium price
from high end online all-night sites
or her desire for ditto replacing what they already have
then the next his drooling over the neighbor's too young
deliciousness while moaning wishes for more
of the same why not I deserve some too plus
look at her engulfing those sweets
treats swallowing gobs of meats Amazon Prime
on demand I'm so angry furious
my tongue hurts my teeth are sizzling

I want to lash out at all of these them he and her
but I'll loll on the sofa and watch that rerun
Rotten Tomatoes 35%
yawn

## Self Portrait as Sea Surge

soft grains of seashells ground

into hot sand

beach born sinking to the earth's center

the beat of surf a rhythm the beat of my life's sway

as if web toed          mouth a gill slit

sea speaking tongues

moan      lurch     calm     break     groan      still

     thrust

reaching land falling back into

ebb      then      flood     next     neap

repeating thrown seaweed glyphs tattooing the shore

         messaging

sand crabs with sea drift

the tufted reeds of beachgrass and dune willow

     salt drying on my forehead       a sweat trickle

green mist and gray gulls

     screech each

         seabed churn undertow deep

threat to breath underwater bursting

     as waves push upswells landward

         rumble lightening pulses

map my internal seas

## Tattooed straight lines not sufficing

I will ink my face
like Queequeg's living parchment a hieroglyphic

labyrinth of enflamed etchings so that looking in a
mirror inverted I can rewind my past searching

each swirl engulfing eyes in an undertow an eddy
churning an aspiration exclaiming dead ends and

blurred attempts my trail of overlapping incisions
and helixes testing the truth of my identity identified

one line intersecting with another serpentine
circumnavigating cutting off/into paths of maybe

where stop starts the journey's wander for me to draw
meandering moments features of feathers and cranes

a wave cresting above seabed churn a cloud in silhouette
against a drop of blood or tear-stained canvas depending

on the light day or night maundering on the skin drawn
not in red desire green need blue despair yellow lust

the trick of the needle's prick blotting smudges of ink
leeching into pores and worn fissures a map of maladroit

missteps like scrimshaw totems each pit scar and facial
flourish a glyphic inflection in transit but black and white

finality decisively unraveling riddles of heaven in earth
earth in shadow then perhaps I could find my way through

straight lines a linear treatise my face a poem rhyming in
ordered stanzas, a grid, pole star aligned with clarity in

couplets or quatrains, comforting scansion, approving
meter but this maze I see reflected reflects myriad

guises more surely the passage of chaos
in ink unspooling

## gasping

air on fire.

embers and ashes.

enflamed swarms ingested.

blackening my skin.

burning my throat.

breathless.

intubation failing to vent.

tongue bit.

teeth ground.

broken nails clawing.

eyes blood torn.

ears burst from fear.

needles puncturing.

gasping.

end stage.

enough.

## Black Spring

Spring melt leads to awakening,
sunflowers emerging in fields,
irises pushing through pavement.
Usually. Not today in blackened Kyiv,
where ice puddles bear tank tracks,
tread marks scarring the land
in this black Spring.

White acacia would bloom
where bomb-ravaged tree shards
now stand skeletal along 1st of May Street.
In a gutter, alongside a blue and yellow
cloth torn and grenade savaged,
gunpowder smudged, swirls an armless doll
draining in the black Spring.

In a suburban housing
complex, bullet strafed, blast pocked,
showered by shell casings,
rising through a concrete crevice,
a Ukrainian crocus buds,
blood red
in the black Spring.

## This Year Darkening

I feel it, this year, as a bird fleeing
with mottled wings from a songless cage.
This year, I feel it, bone cells dying,
necroptosis to amputate.

I see it, this year, words undulating,
hazed as gnawing worms on a writhing page.
This year, I see it, rough boughs of shaking
trees, limbs bowing from age's pillage.

I hear it, this year, a white wind whining
in moans, groans of life's fading umbrage.
This year, I hear it, a faint song singing
of love loss, of life losing, disengaged.

I know it, my rusting clock unwinding
this year, my darkening shroud awaiting.

## In this time of anxiety,

I hide.  From the fear.  My fear of fear.
Fear of touching.  All those virus-besieged
canned goods in the grocery stores.  I'm
scrubbing my hands with antibacterials.
Wearing two masks.  Fear of touching
you, too.  Will you respond?  In kind?
Will you recoil?  As if I'm virus-besieged?
Fear of commitment.  To you.  To my
current job.  Not a career, just a job.
My IDP asks, "What do you want to achieve
this year?  In five years?"  I might as well
write my plans on sand, on a beach, sea-level-rise eroding.
I might as well write my life plans on Snapchat.
Deleted after 30 days if/when unopened.

Fear of failure. Or success.  Fear of wars.  Even peace is
frightening, because then I should be happy, right?  Fear of
high prices. Fear of forest deforestation and floods and
hurricanes and polar ice melt and mortgages and tribal politics
and clickbait and my car breaking down and a tooth cracking
when I have no dental coverage and rogue dogs and road
rampages.  That's me, fleeing, like an emaciated polar bear
from shrinking ice floe to icebergs calving.

Don't even mention cyberattacks on my already low
credit card rating by Russian hackers demanding
cryptocurrency ransoms.  I've never committed a crime.

So I fear police will stop me for some minor infraction. "6:00 p.m. News Flash: man shot while failing to change lanes correctly. Police report that he wasn't obsequious when questioned."

So I hide.
With my pulse ratcheting.
Like 7.2 seismic spikes.
Under fault lines.
And I quiver.
With one eye peeking.
Fearfully.

## Beneath the Sea's Swell the Psyche

She remembered it.  She
remembered it all.
She thought.
It's hard to know
when you wake at 3:00 a.m.,

and your pulse
is cresting like tsunami
surf, and your head pings
like submarine sonar,
like sounding whales

emerging from the fragments
of dreams,
webs of unctuous kelp
slithering between reality
and night shadows.

She thought she saw
herself, first a child in blue,
laughing at laughter,
then herself again, a teen in red,
playing a guitar as if wrestling

electric eels,
then herself, now, a woman
with desires like an ocean's
surge.

The crests were haloed
from the sun. The wave depths
were black, the color
of memory. And each breath, each tidal roll,
peak, valley, trough rising,
crestfallen,

threw upon the shore flotsam,
reminiscences dissipating
like sea spray,
and there, again, she saw, doubt,
a patch of red sargassum invading.

# Recipe for Anxiety

Want to eat some stress? The simple recipe for anxiety starts with living now, in this era, this existential moment of divisiveness, peppered by a past president, a Putinesque tyrant, and ample dollops of fear.

Add to those horrors the following essential ingredients for Anxiety Stew:

1. Obtain 1 lb. of emaciated polar bear steak by trolling through rapidly melting ice floes.

2. Slice the meat into strips and then using baton-wielding police brutality, pound the polar bear meat into compliant tenderness.

3. Cube 3 cups each of carrots, potatoes, and onions, then radiate these vegetables through global warming by placing the cubed ingredients in your kitchen window.

3. Season the meat and veggies to taste as follows:

> •1 heaping tablespoon of salt tears from Ukrainian losses
> •½ cup of pandemic-induced flop sweat
> •¼ teaspoon of antibacterial hand sanitizer
> •a whiff of panic from cyberattacks and cryptocurrency ransom demands
> •2 pinches of jiggling Instagram
> •1 soupcon of oxycontin for flavor

The result: a blood pressure of 170 over 110, a heartbeat of 96, hives, a headache, and a perpetual grimace as you grind your fists into your temples.

Share the results of your anxiety stew with an Instagram photo, write about your worry in a Snapchat post, and join millions of other 21st century survivors by posting on social media this recipe of our common ailment—stress.

## Four Boards Squared

When she trudged from the gravesite, her hands still
dusted with dirt clods thrown, the loss not seared
but gone dormant like seeds in winter chill,
sunk down, burdened with low light and frozen earth,

she wheezed as wind through wooden slats, blades
broken out, nailed back askew.  Her face webbed
as winter dew, mascara misaligned
like exclamation points, smothered screams dampened,

she stepped on November's leaves, hard as steel
shovels biting into frosted clay, tossed
clumps thudding on pine planks to time reeling.
I'm undone, Jim, she moaned.  My path is lost.

One rose on the ground loosed from a bouquet
shone yellow in the lessening light's gray.

# Flayed

That's me on the table pinioned
by angst, my tendons ripped and tied.
I'm sipping ether narcotized
and looking at an Xray of my evisceration.

I see I think a reflection in the surgery room's
halogen lamp, hot as the eighth circle of hell,
my lies of self, and specters come and go,
clothed in bones.

I know I'm somewhere in the blackness of the room,
my teeth gnashing like a metronome,
my tongue swollen in rant and looking at life
through trifocals smudged in delusion.

I'm dressed in old stanzas from another person's poem,
ill fitting. A Rimbaud tie, the waistcoat Apollinaire,
one sleeve Poe, the other Cocteau. And Duchamp shoes
worn on my hands to warm my soullessness.

I look down upon my flayed self to see my heart
tapping like a hammer flailing at nail heads
tap/tap/tap/tap
driven into pine planks.

I bolt upright from the gurney's straps
and roll my sleeves up, my arms tattooed

with liver spots, scrivener's glyphs
demarking my experience without innocence.

And now the end, Byzantium, my hair thin,
my eyes glazed, words on a page through
my trifocals as hazed as worms,
slithering maggots wriggling on a pin.

## Dead

down
slow grow
wooden into
dirt dug fingernails
plank
the shrieking next shroud
worming
stand others circle
chant
down a rope
a rose up red
down

## To mend what roils


the world is roiling in catastrophes
a car that runs each red light stop
and religions speak in indecipherable codes
the text of rants in mumbled slurs
and you think how to find a footing sound
I say embrace me embrace me

leaders of our world engage in
shouted shrill in uncompromised
posturing while storms assail
susceptible lands
and you yearn for footing on solid ground
I say embrace me embrace me

even our families reach but fail
to hold what's firm or find the real
there's illness and age and loss
separation of kind from each in thought
and you hope to help to heal to knit
I say embrace me embrace me

our arms encircling equatorial
in our halves unite the whole
at least this microworld and viral this
and viral that our embracing mends

# Cancer: Triptych

## 1. Shadows and Curtains

The day was sunny late August
and cars drove to locations
expecting to arrive without incident
and I arrived with no expectations
other than good checkup see you next year
then the shadow arrived and my destination
changed and lanes swerved and cars crashed
in my life and I entered a shadow

Each day before was like a curtain
opening to applause and lights shone
and we readied to deliver our lines
to take our places on stage
then the curtain came down the doctor
saying I've got bad news showing me the
Xray my eyes seeing the disease my
mind curtained in its shadow

I feel its presence I know it's there
but time and care and persistence and
endurance and character and strength
raised the curtain and swept the shadow
offstage, but waiting

## 2. Scar

The scar has not healed. I see it every day.
I feel it every way I move, every time I think,

every moment I hope for a future.
It lurks like a specter, this scar, a glare that hurts

my eyes when I look at my children, my grandchildren.
It hurts like a scalpel, this scar, slicing through

my life before, my life now, the swollen skin
a demarcation so that I see

my skin as a parchment calendar scribing
who I was and who I am.

It reads like a road map, this scar, and though
it came from pain, it becomes today,

the person I am, it leads to tomorrows,
the life I'll live, stronger.

The scar has not healed.
I am healing around its wound.

### 3. Still, Always

It's been 19 years since I said
I've got it the mammogram a spider's web
of diseased fear threatening like razors
slicing veins like veins ripped through skin
our family shredded our life as we knew it
a window cracked the glass shards splintering
and then surgery then chemo then radiation
then rehab for 19 years each day a step
through the splintered glass a cut here a cut there
the scars changing from angry red to reminder purple
to memory pink defeated but still on my skin, always

## New Word

I can barely rarely define
today its blast of flash bang
smoke-filled torrent tumbling
upon me like information overload
my brain a dartboard
a liberty bell cracked
with pundits who Dow-crash me
Putin-terrorize me
gasoline-price soar me
climate-exhaust me
I'm crawling with supply
chains all coiled like snake dens
like intestines knotted in pain
What new word could invent to
subsume my global agony
individual despair
existential angst—
a gray cloud eternal 3 a.m. daily hourly
throbbing as pulse as breath obstructed?
What new word can create
the salve needed to placate
    No—to alleviate
       No—to resolve
          No—to uplift
us in this world
our only world
seeking even
a scent of rain?

## Our Prayers

where are the shields
/we need/
to stop the blast
of bullets Glock
and AK
assaults?
that overwhelm the blue
in our veins?
that enter our brains our
schools the bodies
of children with unicorn
backpacks?
that enter
our workplaces inundated
with anger our streets
with late-night drivebys?
church service blood spattered
bibles shredded
commandments torn
as if by raptor teeth
muzzle spit?
while senators say
our prayers are with you?

## Within a Bubble of Breath

It's airborne and drifts within
a bubble of breath the city I exhale
and send to you as a prayer
to ease your strain the stress our
pain this city of hopes contains
no streets with dividing lines no off-
limit postings no curbs nor policed
thoughts no fencing with barbed
emotions no fines for walking
at angles not right a city within a bubble
so small that egos will not fit
instead my breath of inspiration
of wished for habitation
my city that floats as in a wish
contains lampposts of illumination
pets who purr or birdsong tweet
in harmony with schools that teach
to care homes embracing so small that
hatred could never hide behind body armor
concealing weaponry it's a bubble
thus fragile a city of air to breathe as breath
moves from lungs to pulse through veins
to become heart healing analgesic inhaled

Flash Stories

# Them

### 1.  **Her**

The seams of her silk pants edged sharply as a tightened
    garrote.
Her latte eyes, the color of skylines under cloud cover,
    revealed nothing.
All façade.  Within her bones rubbed raw, her blood jumped
    brambles
like rabbits fleeing foxes.

He had done this to her, casting a shadow
like barbed spines of leafless trees
on frozen days.

### 2.  **Him**

He gulped coffee, his veins caffeine-trembling like seismic
    shifts.
His suitcase was half filled:  their baby's tattered bear, one
    eye missing;
a box of seashell shards, gathered before she shared the news;
a torn wedding photo, her eyes shining like Winter ice.

He planned to finish packing
before she returned.
Then he'd leave.

## A Truck in Snow

He parked the truck beneath the oak behind the barn
    across the lake
then handed the keys to his younger brother Hank with a
    backslap and wink,
walked to her and said, "Don't worry, Beth, I'll be fine,
    you know me, always careful,"
and hugged her, kissed her, and turned toward the road,
    a bus waiting.

2004, spring, the oaks in bud, starting to leaf out.  He was
    off to Iraq,
they said, but who ever really knows.  Once on the bus, he
    waved to the family
through fly-speck windows, they waving back, and he was
    gone,  dust pluming
on the country road. Beth wrote daily, at first, and waited.

No news,

but the family said, "he's busy, probably, girl. He'll write
    when he gets a chance,"
and spring became summer.  The truck sat beneath the
    oak, baking in the Kansas heat,
the sun radiating off the truck's red panels, the truck's
    hood pinging in the heat,
like a heart beating.  She wrote weekly, her time taken up
    with chores, and she waited,
and she was pregnant.

No news,

but the local paper reported heavy fighting near Al Anbar,
    where he was maybe stationed,
so the family said, "stay calm, Beth. He's involved.
    He'll be fine. You know him,
always takes care." In autumn, the leaves fell, littering
    the truck with pastels,
leaves stuck to the truck's windows like lost letters. Beth
    wrote weekly, mostly,
but sometimes a month would go by.


No news,

and she was 5 months and showing. The house was heavy
    with quiet.
No one in the family talked about the war, anymore.
    When winter hit, snow covered
the truck, covered the oaks, covered the barn, iced the
    lake, and the farm was iced in fear,
like nighttime chills.


The baby was born after that first snow, a boy they named
    after him, his father
gone to war. Another truck stopped by the house later
    that winter,
and a man got out. He tugged down his khaki dress
    uniform jacket,
straightened his tie and hat, and looked toward the house

with downcast eyes, eyes that were tired from telling tales
   before.
He plodded through the snow with heavy boots.
Before he knocked on the door, Beth opened it, the baby
   on her hip,
her eyes starting to redden like his truck in the snow,
   buried in cold.

News had finally arrived.

# Sepia

They had a barn, pride of possession, poets of old
called it mimesis, so my whiskey-soured professor said,
when wood and fields reflected their green life, reflected
his love for her. Their barn was nailed tight at right
angles, the beams planed straight, hinges oiled, hay
raked. The barn rested in a tended field, spring-alive
from the windmill's well water clear and deep. Apple
trees in their orchard bloomed fulsome. And he tended
the barn and land lovingly, thinking of her with each
nail hammered, each scythe swept, each apple plucked
and polished, under pink skies where even clouds
promised the scent of rain. And he whistled Willie
Nelson's "Always on My Mind." He could see her in
the farmhouse window.

Then stage four arrived like an in-law, a counselor's note
sent home to reprimand, and she was gone, in weeks,
her breathing the rasp of filed metal.

In time the barn's beams swayed in decay, his attentions
distant, his eyes vacant. Doors hung askew on rusted
bolts, stalls echoed as empty as wormed wood, and
mice entered sibilant, filling his void with mischief,
their scurrying feet the chatter of thrown bones. The
windmill shattered, lightning struck, its blades airless in
the farm's dead breeze, and the field's grasses dried like
barbed wire, cicadas screaming in the summer heat.

One dusk, he drank boiled coffee, more dregs than beans, left fried eggs to dry ochre on ignored plates, and packed his truck: their bedspring with splines spent, a bentwood rocker, its wicker seats unraveling, and his Martin guitar, strings sprung, sound hole stuffed with calendar clippings of lost birthdays and anniversaries.

He turned the truck onto a rutted road, dusty with a past harvest's wheat chaff, and left his life, once green, now the color of sunset under cloud-worried skies, the color of sepia.

## Shell

In my youth, we traveled the back roads from Baton
Rouge to Biloxi, Jackson to Monroe, the roads coiling
like a nest of snakes, we four staying each night in a
fleabag motel, paying 31 cents per gallon at one-pump
stations, our '57 Olds, 264,000 miles on the odometer,
sucking gas like a four-pack-a-day smoker, the junk's
hood hooked to the front bumper with baling wire, a
proverb painted on the rear window from Matthew's
"thrown into the furnace of fire," the four of us eating
at drive-ins, greasy chicken or fried burgers: "don't
spill none of that soda on the upholstery," dad would
threaten, "just remember oysters don't spit out pearls
all the time, we don't got money to burn" as he'd drive
from one revival meeting to the next, preaching the
gospel: "oh lord on high, we got sinners among us
who better fear, cuz' hellfire's around the bend," but
around our bend was the red dust and dirt of another
road, another tent, another night in another swaybacked
motel with its parking lot of broken cement, weeds
sprouting through the cracks like dreams awakening
in a nightmare, and him shouting damnation gospel
from Revelation 19 or Thessalonians 1, and now, it all
in a rearview mirror, my eyes squinting in the glare, my
throat scorched from swallowing his perdition, my soul
as empty as a closed roadside diner along a bypassed
road, I think about how cement is made from crushed
shells.

## Not Today

On a gray September, Hurricane Harvey hurtled from the Gulf like an apparition with a scythe. Though still 284 nautical miles from Galveston, waves already lapped angrily against the shore, palm leaves shuddered, gulls shrieked, and red warning flags unfurled against the quickening wind.

"We shouldn't swim today, bro," Larry said with typical caution.

"Come on, man. That storm's days away and look at those waves! We can do some gnarly body surfing," I said with typical teen ignorance.

I was 11 minutes older than Larry, so I won. We dove into the murky surf with undertows and seabed churn waiting like hungry predators.

"Not today," I heard a voice say.

"Why not, Larry?"

"Huh? I didn't say anything. Let's do it if you want."

"Not today," the voice rumbled.

"Stop it Larry! You're creeping me out."

"Seriously, Steve. I'm not talking. What's up with you? Let's catch a wave and go home."

"Not today," the voice insisted.

I looked toward the roiling sky, clouds massed in bruised yellow and green, to find the voice. I looked seaward toward the churning waves to find the voice. I looked inland toward the tidewrack already collecting on the beach, tangled seaweed and broken driftwood thrown by the increasing storm, to find the voice.

"Not today," our father disembodied intoned from under the sea where he died ten years earlier piloting a shrimper squall capsized, his body unrecovered drifting beneath the spines of storm-strewn shipwrecks.

"Hey, Larry. You're right. Today's not the day for a swim. I'll race you home on our bikes."

## Maybe hope

Niki's is dark even on Houston's sunniest summer
days, dwarfed beneath hulking tankers, loomed over
by rusted shipping cranes the size of prehistoric
predators, the humidity a shroud. The Greek restaurant,
frequented by longshoremen, sailors, derelicts, and
denizens of the night, is located just near enough the
ship channel to offer a rare breeze and a quick escape.

I went there for kabobs, bouzouki, beer, and a chance
to breathe danger, to sit close to men and women
with full body tattoos in bad ink, painful piercings still
enflamed, and the scent of despair that permeates the
café like the odor of a mongrel dog on a Houston July.

No one looks into another's eyes. No one asks
questions. You sit, usually by yourself, sheathed in
silence, eat curried food, and wait . . . wait for whatever
might happen next when a summer squall explodes into
lightning along the coast.

But I looked into her eyes, red rimmed with one streak
of mascara raining down her cheek, an exclamation
point to her tale.

She was Albanian, she said in broken English, as
broken as her nails, dirt smudged and ragged. "I'm
Besjana. Means 'belief,' in your language."

"Belief in what?" I asked.

"Don't know, maybe hope, second chance," she whispered, without conviction, as if her words struggled for air, bubbling up from an ocean's depth.

Angry voices across the room flared just then, in one of the dozens of languages spoken in Niki's, and a fight between two crewmen erupted. With the glint of a knife, everyone scrambled for safety as I scanned the room for an escape route.

When I looked back, Besjana was gone. I saw the café's door shut, like a hammerhead's jaw closing on fishermen thrown overboard at sea.

## Llano Estacado

Nothingness. That's what called me like hunger after a fast.

I drove my pickup beyond the county line where the
veil of city haze opened to infinity, the borderless plains
outside Amarillo.

Absence enveloped me. Sound succumbed to space.
Dust plumes replaced people. I could look behind to
see nothing; I could look forward and see no more.

In the miles of distance that only unencumbered land
can create, a crow, separated from its murder, first a
black speck like a worm in my periphery, neared on
the empty air, each flap of its shimmering blackness
bringing the caw's croak, until within range it settled on
a migrant mesquite like a message, dead-eyed staring a
rebuke for my trespass.

"What?" I shouted in defiance.

Silence.

"Get away!" I shooed.

Silence.

I took a step forward, but it matched my feint with a
crooked neck, thrusting its dominance in this domain
of empty land.

"Go" it growled in guttural caw, or so I heard.

I backed off, turned, ran, entered my cab, and sped
toward the city. I sought the safety of strangers numb in
routine, compliant in numbers.

My travel into emptiness scalded me like breathing
the arid air of the Llano Estacado where the wisp of
line between plain and sky snakes circumnavigating,
surrounded by distant sibilance, the hum of expectation,
the moan of despair.

## Lurking

"Davey was just diving, you see," he said, pointing
at the photo lying next to a watermark scarring the
kitchen table where he'd placed his sweating highball
glass now drained.

A cigarette dangling from his lips, he lifted a bottle and
said, "want one?"

"No," I declined.

"Hah," he chortled as if deeply inhaling unfiltered truth
and blew out a plume of delusion. "More for me then"
and poured three fingers of Jim Beam.

"I didn't mean anything, you know. I was just funnin'
him, saying, 'come on, jump, jump, the water's fine.
Look, I'm dogpaddling it's so deep,' though I was
standing on a sandbar." And he laughed again, a squeal
sounding like nails pulled from a coffin.

"You know how kids are," taking a swig of his liquor,
the liquid burning his throat like an acetylene home
brew. He coughed, wiped his eyes, and stared into the
past as if drowning in an undertow. "The twins were
jostling on the pier, waiting their turn.

Sis, as always, a marsh reed filtering sludge, sat off
to the side, wearing red, to stop. She'd warned us all,
whining, 'Don't be diving, you hear.' I don't know
what fear had fed her. Maybe them damn skeeter bites,
maybe some water moccasin thrashing, maybe a squall

we saw earlier that day building in the north, maybe the pier's jagged pilings looking like gator teeth or like a fiend's fingers grasping, but it all enclosed her like a noose. I guess you gotta' believe in ghosts if they speak to you," and he shivered at the memory.

"Anyway, Davey dove, the water too shallow, him barely breaking the water's surface, the dive like a dagger. The coroner said Davey probably didn't feel a thing with a broken neck."

He pulled the highball glass to his lips for another sip. The glass was empty, but one bead dripped down its side like snake venom.

## And the morning sun trailed her bus
in shadows


When she turned 18, it was time, she thought, to find
it, a road, a path, somewhere, anywhere other than West—
West, Texas, that is, population 2,557. Not western
Texas, as she had to explain to any and every yahoo
bonehead from the bigger cities. It's West, that's its
name, damn it to hell, and don't blame me. I didn't
name it! The time had come, time to vamoose, hit the
road, any road, 'cuz anyplace was sure as shootin'
gonna be a step up. So, she packed her duds in an
overnight, stole what cash she could scrounge from
her ma's secret hiding place in the shoebox behind
the Christmas wrapping paper on top of the outdated
*People* magazines growing mold in their attic, and set
off—5:00 am, on foot, toward the Greyhound bus depot
on 2nd and Main, trying to leave the house before her
mom woke for a morning shift at the Sip and Suds
convenience store slash laundromat slash icehouse. Her
dad was long gone, having left for a one-night bender,
fifteen years ago. Walking through the still-dark streets
with only dogs wailing loneliness, moths swirling around
lampposts anxiously, she laid low in the depot's restroom,
then boarded the 7:15 am bus to Amarillo, heading north,
her line of destiny, she thought, traveling the direct path
toward a trade, maybe wealth, or at least something akin
to $7 an hour plus tips, love, who knows, even marriage.
Sitting on the bus's back row, alone, on a brown vinyl
seat cracked like drought-hard clay, she wrote a note to
no one in her diary, decorated with rainbows and hand-
penciled hearts. She was charting a life, the morning
sun trailing her bus in shadows.

## Prophesies

We'd sit in the diner for Sunday suppers, surrounded by
grease fire and bellowed orders for fried chicken and giblet
gravy. Grandpa held court at the head of our table, like
Ezekiel, prophesizing about exile. "I've seen it all, boys,
and it ain't pretty, believe me Almighty, but we got us some
hope, I tell you," crossing his heart, him in his rolled-up
dress shirt, starched as stiff as the gospel, as holey as Palm
Sunday.

With his dinner fork held aloft as a scepter, he'd preach
forgiveness from Colossians 3:13, saying in hushed tones
over his grits, "Bear with each other, boys, and forgive one
another, even if you've got some damned grievance, ya
hear?"

Or he'd lash out at sinners (forgetting all about forgiveness,
I guess). "You remember your Psalms, like 145:20, where
the Lord says He'll destroy them wicked ones," and gramps
would wipe the waffle syrup off his whiskers.

I'd see travelers in the diner come and go like calendar
pages turning, like pilgrims to a shrine. They'd nurse a cup
of dime coffee, their heads bowed over the black steam,
the steam clouding their dreams deferred, and wear work
clothes brown from the land's dirt, as brown as the grease-
fire that hung in the air, brown as a sepia photo in a
family's discarded album.

Their eyes pooled in their coffee cup's reflection, the diner's
harsh light against the night's darkness, their moment of
rest in a worn booth, plastic seats torn like a map, each

crack a destination sought, a path missed. They might
have sought Jeremiah's "good way" and "rest for their
souls," but I never saw any rest in their restlessness,
their alcohol-stewed disturbance, eyes red.

The diner's gone, shuttered soon after grandpa died,
when an overpass was constructed so people could get
someplace else, other pilgrims seeking a new gospel.
And dust settled on the prophesies of my youth.

# Rainbow Triptych

1.

She was six asleep in her bedroom a cuddly bear embraced
and dreams of breakfast donuts her dad had promised the
ones with white icing and colorful sprinkles when a spray of
bullets as warrior wasps tore through the plywood wall tore
through her pink pillow with ballerinas tore through her tiny
skull and blood spat upon her rainbow design of days to
come now churned in red and bitterness

2.

He was dancing with his partner under rhythmic lights and
pounding bass the two entwined in glistening sweat their arms
tattooed with rainbow flags and lost in public privacy en-
shrined by laws protecting self when the gunman burst into
the hall burst through their love and sprayed the walls in
random shots thrown from magazine-fed firearms fit for
combat not street scenes where lovers stroll or nightclubs
where music fails to soothe a murderer's darkening brow

3.

They prayed in pews some kneeling some upright their arms
upraised their eyes closed and whispered psalms their palms
pressed and felt at ease as only those in communion can
surrounded by kin and kindred their prayers for a nation whole
divisions healed guidance for our leaden leaders the bibles
thumbed and pages turned script underlined for passages
adored not imagining not fathoming not understanding how
the intruder upon their prayerful service flinging open the
closed church door screaming epithets of screed could unleash
despite their innocence a rainbow thrash of bullets thrown

## Waxing Moon

From the dinghy he flung the line. It arched through
salt and air, sky as green as the sea was gray, each wave
uplifting the boat's bow. The hook bit deep into the
foam and sank, he presumed, to fathom prey—jack or
snapper, drum or blue.

He laid the pole along his knee, securing the handle
with his left foot, and unwrapped the lunch Charlene
had made, day old bread, mostly heels, with butter and
cheese inside waxed paper, toothpick held, and saved the
toothpick behind his ear.

"I gotta get me one today," he said to gulls overhead,
squawking for his shrimp and shad, in the sloshing
bucket by his hip. "Some to sell at Harper's Bait, maybe
he'll pay me what they're worth, this time, then I'll keep
a couple sprats for Char and the kids, a chowder at least
with some corn or carrots. I'll stick with bread and
cheese, till the sea gives up a tad. This slump I'm in can't
last, I don't think."

He sat, the water in his boat as wet as the sea spray
plastering his hair to his face. He hunched inside his
slicker, holier than Easter Sunday, and stared into the
sky's nothingness, as empty as hunger.

And waited.

The dinghy swirled in the current's eddy, drawing his line
toward the stern, water vibrating on the spiller, droplets
pinging the sea, the sea arrogantly nonchalant as if
wetness mattered to water, as if he mattered to earth.

And waited.

"Damn all I ever do. It goes on around me, and I sit.
Char's back on land, trying to stitch up some cloth,
remnants mostly, and the kids playing in the dirt with
toys I whittled from mossy oak. I'm out here, fishing for
whatever strikes a line. Damn," the wind picking up and
spray hitting him like his low-rent dad with a belt.

"My hitch with Uncle Sam didn't do me no good. I
thought at least me learning how to fix them trucks
would get me out these waters. Uh uh, no sir. Here
I am, stuck like that sonuvabitch, my old man, and his
before him, trying to bring up dinner from bayous and
the swamps. If the weather's good, it's hot as a tin roof
in July, hot as cayenne in etouffee. If the weather's bad, I
might as well be breathing underwater for the downpours
I'm sailing through."

Just then, his fishing pole dipped, he grabbed the handle
like he'd done a million times and started reeling.

"No hurry. Take her slow." He looked north to see land,
now barely a sliver on the darkening horizon, but he
knew where he was, a bit southwest of Grand Chenier,
maybe a mile offshore.

"Low tide's running fast. Gotta reel her in before I'm
pulled too far out. Char'll worry her head off if I'm
not home soon. How long I been out here?" he asked
himself, still reeling. "What's the difference. Just do
the job, like our kind been doing since Jesus was in knee
pants, all of us swampers with silt and seaweed in our
marrow."

He pulled up slack on the line, an inch here, a foot there, as the catch fought. He gave out line to let the catch run a bit but reeled back double, his shoulders hunched, his fists determined. Salt from the air and the sea burned his eyes. His left hand on the rod, his right hand kept spinning.

"He feels like a big one, but gotta do this. Damn fish can't beat me. Not today."

An hour into the struggle, an hour and a half, the shoreline no longer visible, waves crested higher as he rode farther out to sea.

Then he felt the give, the fish tiring, the line rising. He reeled faster, looking back at where land should be, where Charlene and the babies waited.

Another foot, a yard of line, the rod upright to bring the catch closer, then he dipped the rod to gather momentum, pulling the rod upright again and reeling with the savagery of a man fighting centuries of want.

And then the fish broke the surface, thrashed beaten against the boat's hull. It rolled over, a red snapper with one eye glaring.

"God damn, looky that. It's 15 pounds or more, I bet, as good as makes no never mind. Wait till Harper sees . . . no, the hell with Harper. Wait till Char sees it. I ain't selling this beauty for no beggar's change. This here's food for my babies."

He brought the snapper on board, bonged him hard on the head with his mallet, dumped the shrimp and shad bait, filled the bucket with sea water, and put the snapper in to keep it fresh.

Then, he unfurled the sail, used the tiller to turn the boat from sea to shore, and started tacking home into the wind.

"Let it blow out here for all I care," he said, his smile the glow of a waxing moon.

## At Midnight

At midnight, she decided.

He'd come home late, again. Saying, "no more, Babe, I promise. It won't happen, again," just like he'd said last week, the week before, last month, every damn month.

"Trust me, Hon. I mean it," crossing his heart, like a 5-year-old having been caught taking an extra cookie from his mom's sideboard. Like a 10-year-old caught smoking behind the barn. Like a 15-year-old, when I'd bet he crossed his heart as the sheriff arrested him for killing the neighbor's kitten, wringing its neck, then hammering the cat to Mrs. Smith's red oak with four, tenpenny nails.

No more is right she thought, as he stumbled to bed, scratching his ass, kicking his lizard skin boots off.

She was through believing his pleas for forgiveness. She was through imbibing his lies, swallowing them like she'd seen him chug a can of beer, belch, wipe his mouth on his left sleeve, then crush the can. Like he'd crushed her, her trust, her hope.

As she heard him snore, all nasal and congested from his twice-broken nose, she started gathering. She picked up little Bobby, 3 years 6 months, from his thrift store crib, placing him under her right arm while she grabbed his blue teddy with her left. She'd get what she could later.

Then, she and Bobby opened his double-wide's screen door to the driveway, trying to shush the door's bleating creaks, and quietly unlocked her Honda Civic's passenger side to hook him into his car seat. She rushed to the driver's side, jumped in, turned the key, and they were off, probably to her sister Rosalee, two cities to the south.

Her Civic had 257 thousand miles on it, hard driven, maintenance rarely kept up, typical for him, she thought. "Why tend to something when it's easier to just let it die, a price to be paid later, like all his debts," mumbling silently to herself.

She'd left the trailer, though she had wanted to tell him to get the hell out. But that wouldn't have worked. He always said, yelled more like it, when they fought over his drinking, "you don't like it, git gone, girl. This here's my house, my money's paying for it, my sweat been poured while you fetch for the little one." She had no way to counter his diatribe, his height as he loomed over her, his fists, if the drink was alive in him like a nest of coiled cottonmouth snakes.

The car's rear bumper was rusted into cancerous boils from the sea air prevalent around Port Lavaca, southwest of Houston. The bumper dangled about a foot, held on by twists of baling wire. When she drove, the bumper bounced off the road, whining in the two-part dissonance of her life: potholes clanking like punches thrown, corrosion screeching, metal against metal. As she drove, looking once into the rearview mirror, the dawn turned an angry red against the gray sky.

# Gone, a Diptych

### 1. Dead Air

The dust on the road was still. Dead air. Flag dropped.
Leaves waiting.

"Damn, it's hot, hot as sin on a Sunday," I mourned.

"Look, even the windmill blades across the field beyond
the road, they're just intimating water to be drawn like
someone blowing on candles to make a wish, knowing
sure as shootin' wishes don't never come true, not here
at least."

Parked trucks. Metal pinging in the heat.

'Can you hear that? Even the wood on our barn is
creaking groans, yearning for a breeze, like I know
you're yearning, hoping I'll change."

A lop-eared mutt the color of rust dozing in fits. Its tail
disturbing flies. Their movement quick to settle. All
awaiting a breeze. Some hope.

"I'm breathless in your vacuum," she said.

### 2. Cottonwood

"I'm lost," I whispered to myself, taking another swig
from my long neck Bud. The prairie grass whistled
moans in the high winds from the foothills rushing
through the flatlands, rushing through me like images
of you leaving.

"I'm lost," I said, spitting phlegm into the stream moving past me like memories, our home empty, only calendar pages lined through, days removed, our past excised, pages littering the floor with our life's detritus.

"I'm lost," I muttered, biting my tongue, tasting blood. You were as cottonwood, roots seeking deep water, roots foraging through hard clay, my density, my rock-strewn soil untillable, my windblown desiccation, of our landscape.

"I'm lost.  You're gone."

# The Silence

She stood at the window, lace drapes half drawn, the
sky darkening at dusk, darkening under sullen skies,
the sun setting behind the gray hills rising like doubt
beyond the blackening snow.

She breathed out a deep sigh that rattled in her chest
like mice scurrying in the dark and sucked in smoke
from her Pall Mall. Knocking the ashes on the floor,
staring at them as they sifted downward in a slow gyre,
she whispered to herself, "Used to care. Used to keep
the house clean. For them." She had been whispering
to herself a lot lately.

There used to be apple pies on the kitchen countertop,
shiny in red, glazed with sugar. There used to be stews
simmering on the stove, the aroma her life. Now,
neither pies nor stew waited in the kitchen. Sweet and
savory smells had been replaced by dust and ash.

A bluebottle fly hushed against her window screen, the
only sound in her silent house. Her men had gone, the
boys off to cities for jobs away from the land, streets
replacing silos, to carry briefcases instead of hauling hay.

"Gotta go Mom. Ain't nothing left for us here," her
eldest Sam had said, as he waved from his Ford truck,
pulling away from his past, plumes of dirt thrown up
from the road like exclamation points.

Joe, her husband of 43 years, was heart-stopped dead,
the land and farm work whittling him to a nub.

Looking up from the ashes, she stared out her window at the emptiness of her snow-cold land, the empty sky punctuated by crows flying away, black ellipses against the gray clouds.

"Now what?" she asked the silence seeping into her home like chilled air.

## Pale Green and Garnet

Her dress, once green with hope, now pale as roadside milkweed, was washed daily, worn daily to threadbare. She and Don had no money, he said.

"Trying hard, babe. Get up, drive them 60 miles to the oilfields southwest of Houston, my truck chugging on fumes, carburetor dang near corroded on sea salt, work on the rigs under 100-degree heat, sweat dripping down my back like cottonmouth venom, and for what? To drive back to you? For what?"

She lived in his Baytown rental, one room, hotplate, toaster, bed sprung from his weight, stained from his stain, and looked north out the flyspeck window screen, north toward what might be, could be.

She wondered if he'd get an oil strike, wondered if he'd come back flush, though he never had, wondered if he'd come back at all. Hoping he wouldn't.

She'd left Amarillo for the sun, heading south, away from the plain's wind and snow.

"Hey, girl," her friend Sarah had said. "Give it a chance, Hon. What you got to lose? Stuck here, cleaning people's houses, hiding their dirt so they think better of themselves? Go on. Make a life for yourself."

So she did. Left one cold home, ending up in another.

The radio next door to his Baytown rental was on, set to a country/western station, day and night, always playing too loud, accompanied by the clink of beer bottles and an occasional "damn you!" or "hot enough for you?" or sobs. She could hear "Stand by Your Man" through the walls. Same old mewling her mom had cried to. Generations repeating.

"Enough," she said, rooting through the room, looking for a grocery store paper sack for her makeup and empty wallet. She gave the room one final glance, saw in the window's reflection a glimpse of the red welt beneath her left eye, stepped to the door, and flung it open, her eyes cried red, as red as the glass garnet promise ring he'd given her, the one he called a ruby jewel.

## the echo between passing hills


Me


Why can't I have time in your space? Why must I stand
outside looking in through frosted glass? You enter me.
Greedily. Devouring. Taking. I reach, but your air ices.


You


It's a whirr. A sound that I swat away like mosquitoes
hissing. A chilled breeze. An apparition without form.


Me


My ribs are cracking in your vacuum. This want
feels skeletal, slithering through me like lichen, sun
starved. Where is your warmth? Touch? Why does
this always happen, to me. Connections that fray like
severed synapses. Electricity that sizzles then deadens,
narcotized?


You


What does this person want? Always. Clinging.
Cloying. Clawing. You're cacti, and my skin is a rash.
No. Not cacti. Too assertive. You're a pale rose, six
days past the sell-by-date, blackening.

# Love/Loveless

### Act 1. You and me

Filets of trout perfectly browned in warm butter beside
a quartered lemon slice on two Wedgewood plates. A
carrot-sculpted rosette. Two glasses of rosé. Brown,
yellow, blue, orange, red passion. "I'll have iced tea;
she'll have water." The server left us alone to hold
hands in the flickering light of a candle, the shape of
light caressing your face like breezes rustling a redbird's
feathers.

### Act 2. Her

I just want someone. Why can't I find someone? They
come in here every week, sit at the same table, hold
hands, never see me, see only each other, like I'm a
distant noise, a car crash in some other neighborhood,
a solar flare whose eruption won't affect their climate-
controlled environment, a damned iceberg calving,
dissolving into the sea, disappearing into atoms small
enough to be carried on the waves of their love sighs.

### Act 3. Me

You caulk the seams between my stone edges and your
seamlessness. You are chocolate drizzled on my finger
to lick. Let my thumb inscribe circles on your palm to
plot roads we'll travel. Let my tongue touch your tongue
and speak of time and song.

## Act 4. You

You help me see light in different colors. The other
men I've known have been as cataract, their needs
obscuring my vision of self. "Come on, babe, just
this once, I promise." "Hey, get me a beer, won't ya',"
he'd say while scratching his lazy ass. "Let me tell you
what I think." "That chick friend of yours has a big
mouth, always goin' on about her this or that. I mean,
who gives a you know what?!" You listen. You take the
words I speak and weave them into garlands.

## Act 5. Her

Four more hours of this shift. Burning my hands on
hot plates, my soul searing in loss. Then what? An
empty night of Hulu. Bottles of Bud diesel clanking
against my teeth, the sound resounding throughout my
hollow apartment. Endless loops of "Beautiful Pain,"
Eminem screeching in AK-47 staccatos, "Yesterday was
the tornado warning/Today's like the morning after/
Your world is torn in half/. . . It's like an enormous
asthma."

Those two, sitting at the table, eyes fondling each other,
their hands linked like a bridge joining his hemisphere
to hers.

I'm falling, my gravity gone and I'm reeling into ether,
nothing tethering me. Loveless. I want. And my want
echoes.

# Progress

I saw him hollow, my father's substance emptied once returning from the war to inherit our mom and pop corner store from his father-in-law, selling lettuce but not arugula, mushrooms but not shitake, giving credit to neighbors in need.

"Pay me later when you can, no problem," waving to friends from the store door, knowing everyone's first name and their kids' favorite ice cream flavors, how Aunt Rose was feeling after her fall and whether John had gotten his new job.

But the superstore moved in like an eclipse, progress, selling pear infused balsamic, selling more stock cheaper, 24/7, without credit, without recognition of neighbors, undercutting his margins and community like blood draining bruised platelets.

And our corner store sank as a patient amputated into a hospital bed. He then waved at friends as they drove past the door like an open casket, he a widower at a wake, while he sold off perishables, then canned goods at discounts, finally equipment—shelving, meat saws, and grinders, until the store hollowed, became skeletal, the fossilized floor scarred where feet once walked, marred from phantom pain.

I watched him evaporate, the store excised in progress.

# The Existential Sundering of OK Boomer and Gen Z

She says, "we're just a beer joint." Damn right!
Was when grandpa and my pops owned and
served, Dad in Korea, his old man in WW2.

*He says, "the wooden countertops give our joint character."*
*I see each knifed name and profanity as splintered shrapnel,*
*tattoos that need to be lasered.*

See that dollar on the wall? The first tab paid by
boilermakers using our joint to numb their burning
lungs when they finished a late shift at the plant.

*All the wood gives me is a headache from the beer-soaked*
*stench. I'm changing to quartz, adding chrome, painting the*
*place grey, and plastering over Dad's miseries with a second*
*coat.*

And by "beer" we meant Pabst, Schlitz, and
Milwaukee's Best, beers that won our wars, not
kiwi or key lime-infused blonde ales, selling for
$7.50 a pint. My men need good taps at workers'
wages. They paid a price already; I'm not going to
add to their plight.

*My generation wants tapas, craft brews, and Wi-Fi. We*
*want cocktails with Manhattan in the name, or at least a*
*shot at the future with networking. I see an upscale bar*
*with collaborative workspaces.*

Bud was good enough for me and my guys in Nam
when we returned from this or that hooch, a Bud buzz
to buffer ricocheting bullets, to clear our heads from
napalm noise and rotor wash.

*The neighborhood is gentrifying. His working class has moved to
Miami or been stored in old folks' homes with window displays
from Woolworths. Things are just different, and we're not going
backwards to black and white TVs with three stations. I'm
going to install streaming.*

When I got hit by a Cong 7.62mm, the thud of the
slug, the crack of my left arm, still bent like our
grill's spatula, I choppered to China Beach, jetted to
Landstuhl, before coming home.

*His people have been unplugged like their landlines. They're
scarred as LPs skipping beats, unraveled as 80's cassette tapes
stuck in their wood panel Fords. Dad's living in a Cheers world,
but most of his guys have forgotten their own names.*

I got my R&R at Walter Reed, Dad and Grandpa toasted
my return with a Pearl, our joint my haven from PTSD.

*I know there's a war, we're never without one, but "draft" has
lost its meaning to millennials and gen Z. Drink doesn't have
to deaden like Dad's did. Drink can pair with our upscale pub
fare.*

That's what I wanted for my boy Jack. He'd take over
the place, but Afghanistan had different plans. After he
met his IED, he traveled to Landstuhl like me.

*Dad thinks my plans for the bar disrespect the price he paid, the price Jack paid. He's wrong. I'm the next "man" up in our family's legacy.*

We unloaded his Purple Heart and a box of body parts, a DIY kit on how to make a man, with directions only God could fathom.

*The cash register will be gone. PayPal apps and cryptocurrency will replace the crypt where Dad has interred Jack.*

I've got his heart in the cash register and look at it every time a bell chimes. Without Jack, Janie's taking over the bar now. I'm OK with that. Why not? She's my girl, and I want to keep the family birthright going. But where's she going with it?

*I'm changing the joint's name to "Jack's Place," framing that dollar, and Jack's medal will be pinned above the dollar bill that's stuck on the wall like a bug display, curled up in Dad's fetal position, memory askew.*

She's turned her back on the past.

*He's faced the past so long, his future became blurred.*

## Stepping off the edge of earth

Another tempestuous day: a missed tax deadline, my
two-year old spiking a temp hastening a trip to the ER,
leading to a missed departmental meeting, resulting in
a tongue lashing from my peeved boss, ending up with
unpaid overtime to make up the loss.

I got home late. Everything and everyone turned off
and nailed shut, I leaned on my typical panacea—two
Advil and two fingers of double malt. Then I laced my
Nikes, strapped on the Garmin Forerunner, and headed
for the hills to burn off anxieties.

10:00 pm, a shadowed moon, breeze whimpering
through the sycamores lining my route, no light, as
if running through a funnel where gravitational pull
tightened my sinews. Each step I took left me emptier,
a chasm silencing my sorrows, each step leaving me
breathless—pulse slowing, synapses loosened, stress
hollowed.

Ahead loomed my most torturous hill. I trudged,
upward into the maw created by the tree cover, my
running watch ticking time like nails hammered into
wood, like a shovel digging into hardpack: mile one,
one and a quarter, a half. Almost at the top, nearing
the edge, the border between gray pavement and black
air, I felt a twinge, a needle puncturing skin, the twinge

deepening to a hand grasping my arm tightening, then a
hatchet hewing my chest to cleave four boards squared.

My right foot hit the ground, and all darkened as I
stepped off earth, my watch glowing 00.00 in neon
green.

## Sunset diorama

In late August, within the prairie between Lubbock and
Amarillo, when sunset stroked the wheat shafts like banjo
notes, each wave flutter glimmering as weak starshine in
gray dusk, I'd hold dad's hand as we walked the land, our
feet marking progress like notes on a staff, his step bass to
my treble, and he'd hum Vince Gill's "Go Rest High on
that Mountain" in the deep rumble of thunder, or he'd
quote Shakespeare.

"Boy," he'd say, and tousle my hair like wheat straw thrown.
"I seen it all. Cain't complain nary one bit. Yes sir. I've
mewled and I've puked. I've dawdled down our lane to
school like a slug. I've loved, I've lost, I've turned and
tossed, and when I served in Nam . . . I ever tell you
'bout that boy?"

Of course he had, at least as many as the seventeen times
Ulysses sailed the seas to battle in Troy, as often as he'd
recite *Macbeth's* "When the hurly-burly's done, When the
battle's lost and won," but I held my peace and let him speak.

"Sure 'nough son, I soldiered, quick in quarrel, sudden in
spirit, and spied the cannon's mouth. And let me tell you
son, you ain't seen life till you travelled the road with
death, the devil's companion hand."

And dad stopped and stood and wiped his brow with a stained and chambray sleeve, torn from the morning's reaping. He looked left at a herd of heifers, each one cow staring like a Greek chorus, their lowing a soundtrack to his soliloquy. I saw his amber eyes go pale as raw flax seed broken from tallgrass, the tallgrass now windswept around his legs, fronds hurrying past as if time had somewhere to go.

My world might still be a stage with entrances, but his exit was cachectic, he as fragile as the bluestem at our feet drying into darkness in the summer heat.

# The memoir of no one special

Emily Dickinson had it right when she wrote, "I'm
nobody! Who are you?" I don't know why I'm here,
on this earth, now, in this place, just hanging around
like a piece of fruit on a tree, ready to be eaten by
passing bats or fall into foliage and rot, blackening
then disintegrating into decomposed litter. Who is that
person in the mirror looking so much like me? Aren't
we all just atoms, aligned, misaligned, realigning? Why
didn't I live in medieval ages, as a serf, a miller, or a
smith, working in some lord's village in windswept
Northumberland, or a peasant in Mother Russia,
scraping the steppes for potatoes or beets? Why
wasn't I a Neanderthal grunting about the delights
of fire? Why not a soldier at Appomattox or Enzio
or a maiden Mayan sacrificed to satiate the gods? I've
often wondered how my matter wasn't reassembled as
a dung beetle or a carburetor for a 1969 VW bug? As
an atom, couldn't I just as easily have been stardust
spinning around Saturn or a bubble released from
a whale's sounding? Maybe a sludge of hardened
lava spewed from Mt. Kilauea or at least a speck of
paint on Mona Lisa's lips. A strand of hair on Andy
Warhol's bangs? An Insta pic? The sticky-sweet juice
of a bitten kumquat trickling down the chin of some
wanna-be online wish-I-coulda'-shoulda' model? Are
atoms part of sound? I'd have loved being the fifth
note on Mozart's Piano Concerto No. 24 in C minor
or Shakespeare's exhaling "To be, or not." Damn and
blast and bugger it all, as the Brits say. I'm none of
those things, neither sound nor sight, neither here nor
there. I'm nobody, as common as a comma in the *Iliad*
or *Odyssey*, as banal as a forgotten banana left hanging
on a hat rack.

Micro Musings

## a Tweeted Sonnet (280 characters w/ spaces)

sludge ur

high-capacity

multi-clip magazines

shear the firing pins

from all AK 47s

file ur teeth

to blunt ur canines

muzzle ur MAGA fangs

leave bear spray home

& body armor too

break the sharpened

tips from ur flagpole weaponry

sheath your bayonets (pls)

children (& democracy) r onboard

## Bitter on the tongue

like collages of confetti smoldering
these poems send ashes heat-drawn
in updrafts that then drift downward
toward your lips
taste them on your tongue
are they bitter?

## Poems find light through broken glass

The glass web-spidered,
rock thrown and splintery,

once planed and pristine
as lake water unruffled

by breeze dance
reflecting sky silence,

now refracts, the windowpane
tidal as undulating sun shafts,

casting splinters
on the hardwood floorboard.

The shimmer cracks into
facets like rhyme seeking rhythm,

meter imagining theme,
scansion finding a poem

in broken glass.

## Ingesting eclipses

1.

We consume darkness in loss, ingesting eclipses.

When earth and moon fail to syncopate, our axis askew,

Truth becomes dross. Even gilding fails to validate.

2.

Heat-steeped cement, iridescent, turns vapor to flame.

A leaf on the ground colors Fall, mocking with vibrancy.

Mirages fail to satiate, quenching with aridity.

3.

There's no reckoning a mind's cyclonic confusion.

Though we assume, destiny downdrafts in rotating winds.

Clouds move north and south; cicadas siren suffering.

## Adorned

We adorn ourselves
in ailments, worn as medals,
pinned like scar tissue.

## Carbon Based

It's odd to just be
carbon, our intricacies
barely smudged paper.

## Lovers

Shredded, sheared, coupled,
lovers overlay as collage
melding mismatches.

## Life's passage

The fence unhinged swings
like a rheumatoid ambler.
Passage is a trial.

## Miscommunicating

We communicate,
cuneiform conundrums,
like words refracting in water.

## Reptilian Brains

Self-medicated
on our reptilian brains,
why are we surprised?

# Balance

1.

We stand on earth,
Balancing on ether's nothingness,
Striving for substance.
2.

How can we balance
When our axis is shifting?
Norms melt like polar ice.

# Aging

Wavering whispers,
The smoke from the candle snuffed
Remembers flaming.

# Facade

Certitude shatters.
The sound of impermanence
Moans like ice thawing.

## Listening to a Politician

Brayed sound without sense,
Like a flesh-eating disease,
Lobotomizes.

## Enduring Newscasts

1.
Clouds torn from the sky
descend on the horizon
like soot flurrying;
2.
The sky is punctured
and air evaporates.
What masks this despair?

## Endlessly Scrolling

1.
Fingers tap and scroll,
flitting from site to site like
oxycodone birds.
2.

Rather than confront
the world, mainline technology
to anesthetize.

## Fear

1.
Midnight fears shatter
like a knife splintering bone,
fracturing psyche,
like candles snuffed
smoke engulfing.
2.
We need to carry
lamps when darkness overwhelms,
upraised hands signaling
"Slow down, stop, I surrender,"
please, I've had enough!

## Get Real!

Past is purposeless.
Retrieving a falling star
Denies gravity.
But past can become new,
Like an empty house for sale.

## Experience Should Teach

1.

Concentric circles
scar the moon.  Craters reflect
strength after impact.

2.

The line between was,
is, and could be promises like
a pulsing heartbeat.

3.

Though stasis comforts,
permutations design pearls,
pressure's recompense.

## Where to find strength

1. When tensions create
an emotional maelstrom,
what grasp tethers us?

2. Reach deep.
Most of earth
is under water.

3. Marred, scarred, seamed, stitched, life
suffices.  Though not pristine,
being breathes wonder.

## As We Near Complete Destruction

On the empty day in early
spring when we ran from fear,
I looked back on the virus near
and saw my child's nightmare—

a dream distorted like a cat afire
with fleas dancing a derelict jig,
the flame escaping heat into cold,
expiring on blackened fur.

**Dr. Steven M. Gerson**, Professor Emeritus, Johnson County Community College, was named 2003-2004 Kansas Professor of the Year, chosen by the Carnegie Foundation. He is the co-author, along with his wife Sharon Gerson, of 13 college-level textbooks and the author of *Once Planed Straight: Poetry of the Prairies* (Spartan Press-KC) and *Viral: Love and Losses in the Time of Insanity* (Spartan Press-KC). He has published over 200 poems in many journals and was named a finalist for the 2021 Poetry of the Plains & Prairies (POPP) Award. Steve is most proud of his 50+ year marriage to Sharon, for whom all his love poems are written, his wonderful family of Stacy, Stefani, and Rob, and for the joy of spending time with his three grandchildren: Sophia, Samantha, and Jacob. These people are the poetry of Steve's life.

This project was made possible, in part, by generous support from the Osage Arts Community.

Osage Arts Community provides temporary time, space and support for the creation of new artistic works in a retreat format, serving creative people of all kinds — visual artists, composers, poets, fiction and nonfiction writers. Located on a 152-acre farm in an isolated rural mountainside setting in Central Missouri and bordered by ¾ of a mile of the Gasconade River, OAC provides residencies to those working alone, as well as welcoming collaborative teams, offering living space and workspace in a country environment to emerging and mid-career artists. For more information, visit us at www.osageac.org

Osage Arts Community